TRID: The Future Of Real Estate Is Now!

About the Authors

Dean Wegner

Consumer Finance Expert Dean Wegner is a leader in housing with over 20 years of experience. Dean is Sale Manager for Academy Mortgage Corporation in Scottsdale, Arizona. Dean is a member of 25 financial organizations and a Certified Consumer Credit Counselor. He has spoken to the media about housing over 1,000 times, including cover stories in The USA Today and appearing on CNBC's "On the Money". Dean is also an accomplished author and his recent release "Life After Foreclosure" is available in bookstores nationwide.

Dean owns a Real Estate School and wrote the 255-page guidebook, "How to Pass the Arizona Real Estate Sales Exam".

His community involvement includes being a Rotarian, a Board Member of Big Brother Big Sisters of Arizona and a founding member of Uncle Skate Charity. Dean lives in Arizona and enjoys spending time with his three wonderful daughters.

Kevin Hardin

Kevin W. Hardin is Director of the Mortgage Mediation Group at McCarthy Law PLC and an Arizona licensed real estate agent. The Mortgage Mediation Group assists homeowners with issues related Short Sale, Loan modification, Foreclosure, Deficiency, RESPA, TILA and Post Foreclosure related claims under the California Homeowner Bill of Rights. As a licensed real estate agent, Kevin's practice becomes a one stop shop.

In 1983 Kevin joined the Air Force and after active duty reenlisted in the Air National Guard and attended New Mexico State University. Kevin obtained his real estate license at that time and began working in real estate while going to school.

Following Operation Desert Storm and completing his National Guard service, Kevin graduated from New Mexico State University with a Bachelor of Science in Sports Medicine and moved into the Real Estate Mortgage Regulatory and Statutory space where he worked for 16 years.

More about Kevin: http://kevinhardin.com/

Disclaimer and Terms of Use: Effort has been made to ensure that the information in this book is accurate and complete, however, the author and the publisher do not warrant the accuracy of the information, text and graphics contained within the book due to the rapidly changing nature of science, research, known and unknown facts and internet. The Author and the publisher do not hold any responsibility for errors, omissions or contrary interpretation of the subject matter herein. This book is presented solely for motivational and informational purposes only.

Table of Contents

INTRODUCTION:

The American Dream—own your home, good job, spouse, and two-point-three kids in a white picket fenced yard with a dog and a cat. Many of us dream of such idealistic living. We are told that in this land of the free that it is completely attainable. Children are told from a young age that if they work hard and get a good education, life will fall into place. What our children are *not* told is how confusing all of this stuff can be. I know that when I was a child, no adult told me about the process to getting a home loan, credit, my FICO score, or even how to apply for a basic loan. This is something that has plagued the minds of generations of adults as they transition from those blissful days of blanket forts and crayons.

Before one can even begin the actual process of purchasing a home with a mortgage, one must become familiar with some basic terms. There are several different types of mortgages. These types of mortgages are listed as follows: fixed rate, balloon, adjustable rate, interest only and two step mortgages. Many sub-categories find themselves among these four primary types of mortgages, but these four are the most common.

A fixed rate mortgage is a mortgage that has an interest rate that does not change. Three-fourths of all homeowners apply for this type of loan and opt for the thirty-year repayment term. However, the downside to the thirty-year repayment term is that the fifteen year repayment term tends to build equity at a faster rate.

What is equity? Equity is a term that most people hear but do not quite understand. Sure, it is easy to define. Merriam-Webster Dictionary has the definition "the value of a piece of property (such as a house) after any debts that remain to be paid for it (such as the amount of a mortgage) have been subtracted." The words are not difficult to find, but what does it *really* mean? In regard to a home loan, equity is the amount your home is worth based off of what you have paid on the principle of the loan as well as the current market value of the home in question. Some people, in order to finance major expenses such as college tuition, get loans against the equity. This means they borrow money against the equity built by money they have already paid on their home. Yes, most would agree that this idea is not the most intelligent of concepts, but it happens more often than not. The concept of an equity loan just proves that if someone invents it, someone will buy it.

To continue on our short lesson on types of mortgages, let us define what a balloon mortgage is. A balloon mortgage is a type of loan that can have the same term as a fixed rate mortgage, but there is a requirement that it must be paid off prior to the end of the term. The occurrence in a balloon mortgage is simply this: monthly payments are small and there is a large payment, often referred to as the 'balloon payment', at a set date.

An adjustable rate mortgage is a type of mortgage that is pretty much self-explanatory. With the first payment, the interest rate is fixed until a set period of time, where the interest rate will adjust and the payment will change. Following this change, the interest rate will again be fixed, but for a short period of time till the next adjustment. For many borrowers, this can become confusing and sometimes lead to surprises later in the term of the mortgage

Adjustable rate mortgages are very similar to two-step mortgages. In fact, the two-step mortgage is a type of adjustable rate mortgage. What occurs here is that the rate of interest is fixed for one half of the term and then changes for the second half of the term. This gives the consumer more 'wiggle room' in regard to the amount of repayment.

Interest only mortgages are mortgages that have an initial period where the payment is based only upon interest owed and no principal is paid. At a set point, the interest only period will expire and the payment will then increase according to the remaining term of the mortgage in order to be paid off in full by the original term.

For the last 30 years, , the law has required that two specific disclosure forms to be provided by lenders when consumers apply for mortgages. One form is called the Good Faith Estimate (GFE) and this form and the Real Estate Settlement Procedures Act (RESPA) dictates its content. RESPA was enacted in 1974. RESPA was enacted in order to reign in abuses by the real estate industry that was increasing costs for consumers. The other form is called the Truth-in-lending (TIL) disclosure. This form introduced the concept of Annual Percentage Rate (APR) in 1968 as part of the Truth-in-Lending ACT. In addition to that, another two forms were required upon the official closing of the loan. The reason this law was created was to protect consumers from lenders who may or may not have wanted to be dishonest in their dealings. This law also required banks and other lending financial institutions to disclose the information regarding interest rates prior to processing a loan application or beginning a loan process.

In an effort to protect the consumer and make the consumer much more informed, the consumer became even more confused. It was very difficult for lenders to reconcile the TIL disclosure with the GFE. In addition to this, since these two forms are required to be redisclosed at the closing of the mortgage, the confusions would grow as changes were made. Though they say essentially the same thing and spell out exactly what is expected of the consumer and the lender, the language used is not 'user friendly'. It is highly inconsistent. Even lenders and real estate agents find the forms difficult to explain and would rather not have to provide them at all due to this one reason—they are entirely too complicated. In an effort to solve this confusion, new forms have been introduced under revisions to RESPA and TILA that will change the industry forever.

Chapter One:

When people hear of the 'Great Depression', they often conjure up vivid details acquired in history class or through experience of a time in the history of the United States that multitudes were unemployed and outlook on life was bleak. Franklin Delano Roosevelt's 'New Deal' was seen as what saved the country from slipping into status as a third world country. Yet, the United States of America has seen many other 'depressions' and 'recessions' in the short time between the 1930's and now.

The 1970's had the gas shortage. Consumers would have to ration their gasoline usage, and this prompted automobile developers to create more fuel-efficient engines. The 1980's saw two financial crises. One occurred in 1980 and another in 1987. Both crises contributed directly to the debt crisis in Latin America, the savings and loan crisis in the U.S, and also led to extreme liberal economic policies over the next two decades.

However, one of the more recent economic recessions, or financial crisis, that has been seared in the minds of the world is the Great Recession of 2008. This particular recession has been dubbed *the* worst global crisis since the Great Depression. Many larger financial institutions were in danger of collapsing. Stock markets plummeted. The worst part of this, however, hit the general population directly as the housing market toppled over. Many people were evicted from their homes or foreclosed upon. The unemployment rate rose sharply as many companies downsized or shut down altogether.

The United States was not the only first world country affected. Great Britain and much of Europe struggled with a crisis involving the sovereign to debt crisis. Many people blame society's inability to restrain themselves in using credit or the fact that many people live a life of instant gratification with little regard to consequences. However, it had nothing to do with the perceived ills of society. BNP Paribas terminated withdrawals from three hedge funds. If you recall, BNP Paribas is a French based bank and one of the largest banks in the world. For them to stop the flow of any sort of funds without due cause can have horrible effects on the global economy, as it did in this case.

Young adults grow up and are told that investing in land is the most solid investment they can make. However, the reality of this is that no investment is one hundred percent guaranteed. This was proven when just three years prior, the housing 'bubble' in the United States exploded—and not in a positive way. Everything that had been tied to land and real estate was nearly decimated. This crisis was caused by the complex system of mortgages and the politics involved.

Just prior to this crisis, policies existed that made the 'American Dream' of home ownership seem so simple and desirable. Loans were easier to get, which led to the acquisition of subprime mortgages, because it was believed that the value of the homes would only go up rather than continue to fluctuate as history suggested. Though it wasn't illegal, there were also 'sketchy' dealings in regard to trading practices by both buyers and sellers in regard to homes such as the The Federal National Mortgage Association (Fannie Mae) and the Federal Home Loan Mortgage Corporation (Freddie Mac) scandal. In addition to all of that, banks did not have the amount of money required to actually back the deals they were making. In short, the banks were 'writing checks their rear ends could not cash'.

Once all of this came to light, investors no longer had the confidence in the institutions as they once did and began withdrawing their support. This lack of confidence in the banks had a significant impact on the world's stock markets. The years 2008 and 2009 saw the most financial losses. Many of the world's economies began to slow down. Credit was more difficult to come by and trade between countries slowed down as well. This meant that many countries who relied upon export suffered first, but this only was the height of the ripple effect through the world's economies.

To respond to this, the United States of America passed the American Recovery and Reinvestment Act of 2009. This was a fiscal stimulus that outdid all other stimuli as it bailed out the banks rather than distributed funds to the American public as had previous stimuli.

Such a major financial crisis is not allowed to occur without some sort of investigation. The saying goes that if one is aware of history, it is likely that one will not repeat those mistakes. This is true in some cases, but not all. However, there was an investigation into this particular financial crisis completed by Carl Levin and Tom Coburn who were both United States Senators at the time.

During their investigation, it was revealed that the reason for the crisis involved several different factors including, but not limited to: conflicts of interest not revealed to the public, lack of regulation, the credit rating agencies, and the in ability or lack of effort to control the excess of Wall Street itself. This crisis was completely avoidable, according to the report, as so many agencies 'dropped the ball'. In addition to simple failures, there was a lack of ethics involved as well as zero accountability.

Another event created the foundation for this crisis to occur. In 1999, the Glass-Steagall Act was repealed. This action removed the one thing that separated the investment banks and the depository banks. Banks could now invest their depositors funds into risky investments. The Glass-Steagall Act had been in place since 1933 as part of an effort to pull the country out of the results from the 1929 stock market crash. It was said that the reason for the stock market crash in October of 1929 was because depository bankers became "overzealous" with the investments of their clients' funds. So, the Glass-Steagall Act of 1933 created a barrier of sorts and also created an insurance system to ensure deposits remained safe—thus, the beginning of the FDIC. In essence, the government now would oversee the banks' dealings in regard to how their clients' money was handled. However, once this act was repealed in 1999, the FDIC still existed, but its power was severely restricted. This re-created the scenario in 2008 that caused the Great Depression in 1933.

Chapter Two

More about The Great Depression of 1930's and Great Recession of 2008

Prior to the crash of 1929, there was great speculation by the bankers in regard to certain, but highly risky, stocks. The same behavior happened between 2003 and 2007 in regard to the housing market. This speculation was caused because many states had been witnessing major increases in housing prices, which led to a greater return on investment for those who had purchased prior to that.

During the years preceding the Great Depression, the stock market was not regulated the way it is today. At the time of the 1920's, people were able to purchase stocks on margin. This meant that only a small percentage of the cost of the stock was put down in cash. For example, let's say that in 1925, a person purchased $1000.00 worth of stock. That person would only have to actually put down $100.00. If the stock increased by thirty percent, their actual investment would have tripled, but he or she would have reaped 300% of the rewards if they were to cash in the entire stock. Where was this extra money to have come from? If everyone was purchasing stocks on margin, then the money was not there to pay should someone 'cash out'. This 'wild speculation', as it was colloquially referred to, led to high prices. However, those prices were imagined, not real. There was no actual financial backing to those prices. When Americans at that time of the Great Depression panicked and cashed in their stocks to avoid any kind of loss, almost overnight, the stock market crashed completely.

Because the banks were failing, people lost confidence in the economy. People became frugal and stopped spending money unless it was necessary. In addition to that, the unemployment rate was at twenty-five percent by 1933.

Similar things happened during the Great Recession of 2008. However, it was more geared toward the housing market in 2008 than the stock market. The similar type of greed led to people purchasing homes with mortgages that they could not afford with no ability to financially back their purchase. The banks were involved because of the loose lending practices and lack of upholding credit standards. Again, citizens and banks were speculating on how the housing market would do and failed to realize the basic laws of gravity apply to the world of finance as well.

In addition to the housing market collapse, the unemployment rate rose drastically as well. Though it did not raise as high as twenty-five percent, it did climb to fifteen percent in some states.

The Great Depression happened in October of 1929, but why did it take until 1933 for the government to respond? During this time, Herbert Hoover was the President of the United States. His actions proved him nothing more than a figure head since he did nothing more than sit there upon his perch doing nothing. However, it took the election of Franklin Delano Roosevelt and his 'New Deal' ideas to begin changing the state of the country.

President Barack Obama came in to the scene in 2008 with roughly the same approach. Both presidents introduced many changes to regulations to avoid the same thing from happening in the future. Each one also attempted with their best effort to calm the fears of the general public. Unfortunately, Obama's version of the 'New Deal' has cost taxpayers trillions of dollars. Many Americans resent this modern-day 'New Deal'.

As part of Roosevelt's 'New Deal', the Federal Deposit Insurance Corporation made its way onto the scene. This 'corporation', which is actually part of the United States Treasury, ensures that one's deposits are insured up to a total of $100,000.00. Obama raised that amount to $250,000.00 in 2008 to bolster consumer confidence.

In addition to taking other measures, Congress passed the Dodd-Frank Wall Street Reform and Consumer Protection Act of 2010 (Dodd-Frank) which President Barack Obama signed into law.

Chapter Three

Now that you have a little bit more of information regarding the terminology in the world of mortgages, let's discuss the Dodd-Frank Act and TILA-RESPA INTEGRATED DISCLOSURE ACT and how it affects the 'American Dream' of homeownership.

The Dodd-Frank Act was officially signed in July of 2010 and brought with it a multitude of changes to all federal financial regulatory agencies that were going to take several years to implement. One of those changes was the Volker Rule

The Volker Rule became effective on April 1, 2014. This 'rule' is very similar to the Glass-Steagall Act of 1933, though the initial revisions to regulations on banks in the original passing of the Dodd-Frank ACT was watered. In the 'watered down' version, there were just a few changes restricting risky behavior of banks. Rather than restricting depository banks from making any risky investments, it allowed those banks to invest three percent or less of what is called 'tier one' capital in hedge funds and the like.

The original restriction on banking activity was called the "Bank and Savings Association Holding Company and Depository Institution Regulatory Improvements Act of 2010". These restrictions were referred to as the 'Volcker Rule" . The restrictions were originally proposed by Paul Volker, American economist and former Chairman of the US Federal Reserve. It restricted the relationship that often happened with those that owned the bank and those that operated the hedge funds. It restricted US Banks from making certain kinds of speculative investments that do not benefit their customers. Often, in these types of professional relationships, the full extent of that relationship is not disclosed to any sort of regulating entity and a conflict of interest often tends to occur.

The Dodd-Frank Act is broken down further into sixteen different sections or Titles. It requires over twenty-two periodic reports to regulatory agencies in order to oversee the different financial markets. The end goal was to promote financial stability in the United States and give transparency to the entire financial system. Prior to the collapse of the housing market, three different 'economic stimulus packages' have been passed to attempt to relieve the strain the economy was suffering at the time. The Dodd-Frank Act sought to end bailouts and to keep financial services from abusing the system by altering the entire existing regulatory structure. In this, more agencies were created and others were either merged with one another or removed altogether. It sought to create order where there was chaos. Prior to this, there were many opportunities for oversight which posed a significant risk to the operations of the Federal Reserve Act. The bottom line was that it was needed to protect the American consumers from corporate greed.

How the Dodd-Frank Act Changed the Financial System in America

The Dodd-Frank Act has affected many aspects of the financial world in a multitude of ways. For example, the SEC Office of Credit Ratings was established in order to oversee the credit rating agencies. The reason for this was that many credit rating agencies were not giving accurate information in regard to a consumer's credit rating. This was one of the direct contributors to the Great Recession of 2008 and the bursting of the housing market as consumers were applying for loans for homes. With the establishment of the SEC Office of Credit Ratings, the credit reporting agencies are now accountable to ensure the accuracy of the information of consumers whether those consumers are entities or individuals.

The idea behind the Dodd-Frank Act is that it will prevent the country from experiencing another Great Recession/Great Depression. However, it has many critics who have analyzed the same information. Logically, the 'New Deal' and the Glass-Steagall Act of 1933 was meant to do the same thing, yet the economy has suffered many setbacks since then that could be considered a major crisis.

Those who are in full favor of the new laws signed into act by President Barack Obama, then there will be absolutely no worries. Yet, it seems that the idea that nothing bad could happen is the belief of an idealist.

Those against the Dodd-Frank Act feel that its failure will cause worse circumstances than before the act was passed. They also believe that it will affect the United States standing in trade and competition globally. It is an act passed by the same people who failed to prevent the crisis of 2008, so why should they be trusted. In addition to that, the new agencies created will require funding which will come from the tax paying public.

Chapter Four

TILA-RESPA INTEGRATED DISCLOSURE ACT and
Mortgages—Past and Present

To apply for a mortgage, a person must first go to a mortgage lender to begin completing paperwork once he or she has chosen a home that he or she wishes to purchase. With most homes costing anywhere from $100,000 and up, it is highly unlikely that anyone can pay this amount of money all at once in cash—hence, the purpose for mortgages.

Before, mortgages involved long and complicated steps. Terminology is used that can befuddle the consumer who has mistakenly trusted the loan officer handling the mortgage. What the consumer fails to realize is that the loan officer makes a commission on every mortgage, regardless as to whether it is ever successfully paid or defaults.

In 2007, the housing market came to a screeching halt. It was discovered that many loan institutions were abusing the system. The Federal National Mortgage Association (Fannie Mae) and the Federal Home Loan Mortgage Corporation (Freddie Mac) were part of that abuse.

Fannie Mae and Freddie Mac bring the primary source of what is called 'liquidity' to the mortgage industry. Fannie Mae and Freddie Mac are what are called Government Sponsored Enterprises (GSE). Following the collapse of the mortgage market in 2007, Fannie Mae and Freddie Mac were taken into conservatorship by Federal Housing Finance Agency (FHFA) a federal agency. Though still private, they are now controlled by the government. They purchase mortgage loans from the private sector, secure those loans, and guarantee payments of both principal and interest to those external investors. Both Fannie Mae and Freddie Mac held some of those loans purchased for their own investment purposes as well.

Once Fannie Mae and Freddie Mac purchased these loans, this freed up capital on mortgage lenders' balance sheets allowing them to make more loans to more consumers. The purchasing of these loans by Fannie Mae or Freddie Mac meant that the loan was guaranteed should the consumer default on their mortgage. This meant that investors did not have to concern themselves with the risk of the consumer's possible default and credit risk. The American Dream was now available to the majority of American families since the 1970's.

Wall Street observed the success that Fannie Mae and Freddie Mac were using, they began purchasing mortgages for their own purposes and created a major shift in the mortgage market.

When the housing market collapsed in 2007, the blame was primarily distributed among Wall Street, Fannie Mae, and Freddie Mac despite the fact that the latter two had very little to do with the actual collapse. The burden of blame lies primarily with Wall Street. The reason? Wall Street began taking on a function outside of their assumed jurisdiction. They began selling large quantities of high-risk or exotic mortgages such as adjustable-rate mortgages which included balloon payments and contained negative amortization.

The two worst offenders on Wall Street were Lehman Brothers and Bear Stearns. They managed to use the loopholes in the credit-rating system through the agencies like Moddy's, Fitch and S&P to pass these high-risk investments off to misinformed investors under what was known as a 'private label mortgage security'. This 'private label mortgage security' meant that the mortgages in question were not backed by Fannie Mae or Freddie Mac and had no actual backing at all other than the word of Wall Street.

Despite receiving the largest portion of the blame, both Freddie Mac and Fannie Mae lost more than they gained as the housing bubble grew just before exploding. By 2006, both Freddie Mac and Fannie Mae only guaranteed approximately thirty percent of the market share. However, their mistakes came along in 2007 when they began also investing in subprime mortgages based on the ratings of these credit rating agencies deemed 'low risk' without realizing the risk assessments were lackadaisically completed and not accurate.

Another mistake that both Fannie Mae and Freddie Mac made was to change the restrictions on their underwriting practices. Both establishments had a classification of loans they called Alternative Agency Loans (Alt-A). Those loans went to those who were deemed 'low risk' with excellent credit and debt to income ratios and higher incomes. The problem with this was that they required very little proof of one's income. This created a gaping hole in the system, which opened the door to major fraud on the behalf of the mortgage originator who is trying to secure the loan by any means necessary as that is from where he or she profits.

Fannie Mae and Freddie Mac's failures were simply "bad business decisions" backed by "insufficient capital" along with lack of diversification in business. It is a good business practice to hold more than one line of business just in case one source fails.

By the time the peak of the housing market crash in the latter part of 2007, Fannie Mae and Freddie Mac lost over $265 billion. They were left 'holding the bag', so to speak, by Wall Street as Wall Street abandoned the mortgage market in the United States leaving investors high and dry. The government stepped in to save the day and placed both entities under government control after deciding the complete failure of Freddie Mac and Fannie Mae would paralyze the entire economic system of the country and possibly the world.

Today, both Freddie Mac and Fannie Mae are doing very well. However, they are still in conservatorship and Congress is still discussing privatizing the GSE's to protect the public from this risk happening again.

Chapter Five

Breakdown of TILA-RESPA INTEGRATED DISCLOSURE ACT

Finally, we have reached the point you have been waiting for—the official break down of TILA-RESPA INTEGRATED DISCLOSURE ACT (TRID).

The primary function of TRID is to simplify the mortgage process and streamline the forms to protect the consumer and the market from those who sought to profit from possible high-risk investments that led to the housing market crash of 2007. The actual law provides a solid explanation of the forms, how they should be completed, and the purpose of those forms.

The first form to be completed is the Loan Estimate (LE). This form replaces the Good Faith Estimate (GEF) and Truth-in-Lending (TIL) disclosures which outlines the estimate of fees in the closing of the loan itself and lays out the annual percentage rate and the cost of financing the home over time. Rather than have some mortgage loan officer ramble through the technical details as he is pushing a pen in your hand and papers in your face begging you to sign, it requires that every detail of the costs versus risk as well as major elements of the loan be spelled out intricately during the loan acquisition process. Mortgage companies are required to have this form in the consumer's hands no more than three days from date of application or six days if it is being mailed to them.

The second form to be provided is the Closing Disclosure (CD). This form replaces the HUD-1 Settlement statement. This form must be delivered 3 days prior to closing. No longer can we have closing table surprises with interest rates changing or fees going up. The lender is responsible for issuing this form and the mortgage cannot close prior the 3-day period. Giving consumers the time to study and understand what they are signing.

Before TRID, consumers were often unaware of the key elements involved in the closing costs. They were confused when it started and even more confused and angered at closing when the terms of the loan were changed at the last minute. Once TRID is fully implemented in August of 2015, consumers will be required to be informed of all key elements in calculating the closing costs. It also assists consumers in deciphering the affordability of the loan giving them another opportunity to compare with other loan offers before signing on the dotted line.

What happens if there is a change? There are three triggers that would require a lender to start the disclosure process over with the LE. 1) The addition of a pre-payment penalty; 2) A change in loan product i.e. changing from fixed interest rate to a variable interest rate, etc; and 3) If the Annual Percentage Rate (APR) goes up by more than One Eight Percent (.125%) on a fixed rate or One Quarter Percent (.250%) on a variable rate.

So what about fees and costs? The CD incorporates the fees and costs (finance charges) into the APR. That is how a consumer can gauge the cost of borrowing. If your APR goes up, then your fees have gone up and you should ask what fees changed and why. If one of the three triggers are met, the mortgage originator must re-disclose a LE and must wait three days after delivery before issuing a new CD. The CD has an additional three day period after delivery before the closing docs are issues. This might delay a closing, but will ensure the consumer is protected form surprises and misinformation. Buyers, Sellers and borrowers in refinances, will still get a closing statement like before referred to as the Combined Closing Statement (CCS).

TRID will not affect those who are seeking lines of credit based on equity, mobile homes not being purchased as part of a land/home package, or 'rent to own' agreements as those individuals are not considered to be creditors and do not typically report to the credit agencies.

TILA-RESPA INTEGRATED DISCLOSURE ACT and the Future of the Housing Market

As of today, and since 2009, the United States Treasury Department now backs every single home loan made. This kind of financial support is not logistically sustainable, as our economic infrastructure simply was not built for it. So, what is America to do in order to make a smooth transition from government backed mortgages back to having them guaranteed in the private sector?

Since the government took control over Fannie Mae and Freddie Mac, many groups have attempted to provide answers to the questions posed by consumers. Many believe that there needs to be some sort of accountability to the government through transparency, but that the government cannot fund totally that transparency.

The Center for American Progress devised and subsequently released its plan for handing the reins back to the private sector in regard to the housing market. The Center for American Progress believes that there needs to be more consistency and access to the credit system, more stability, more transparency and standardization in laymen's terms, and more access to more people.

So many people ride the fence over their beliefs on this one. Conservatives tend to focus on the causes of the crisis, citing the rhetoric is false, and claim the best way is to make the mortgage market completely run by Wall Street. However, history proves that it is not simple rhetoric as it was the private sector of Wall Street that caused the housing market to crash in the first place.

Let's turn to history and let it guide through facts. Back in the 1930's during the Great Depression and before government backed anything in the mortgage sector, most mortgages were short term with high down payments—usually fifty percent or higher. Loans were often called due to panic, which meant those with loans had to pay it all upon the calling of the loan or risk being foreclosed upon.

If government stepped out of mortgages completely, it would most likely mean that fixed rate mortgages would become a thing of the past. Many middle class families would not have the access needed to get a home loan. In short, we would be repeating history. Considering the state of the country at the time of the Great Depression and the fact the economy was only improved upon due to the needs of World War Two, we must as ourselves—do we really want to go down this road again?

Final Chapter and Closing

What This Means for Consumers

What does all of this mean for the consumer? Granted, there are a lot of details in this book. Mortgages are complex and risky, but with the new regulations in regard to RESPA, TILA, TRID, the process is more streamlined and there is more transparency. Prior to TRID, many of the forms confused consumers. This caused consumers to take an 'I'll just make my payment and hope all is well' approach. This is wrong. Consumers need to be involved. It's your money.

We have new forms for consumers. These forms come with a time frame in which the mortgage originator must comply with when delivering to the consumer. Several confusing forms have been combined to streamline the process as well as provide more simplified language. This means the 'fine print' will have to have proper explanation or be re-worded to fit the true intent of the mortgage originator.

Also, vital information to the consumer's benefit will be required to be highlighted such as interest rate, annual percentage rate, total monthly payment, and total closing cost. All this will be required to be on the first page making it highly unlikely to be missed by the consumer. In addition to that, information on taxes, insurance, and the interest rate must be provided in respect to how the payments could be altered in the future. This is something not previously disclosed and assist consumers on making a truly informed decision as to whether he or she can afford the mortgage in the first place.

In addition, there will also be highlighted warnings about any pre-payment penalties. These penalties could be such as paying off the entire loan early or adding to the loan balance. Cost estimates of services provided also must be included in the paperwork.

With every new law or change to a law, there are always lists of what is and is not allowed. Lenders are not allowed to increase their charges for the duration of the loan unless the consumer asks for a change in services or if the information provided by the consumer becomes inaccurate.

Consumers also have a responsibility to provide accurate information so that the lenders can perform their duties of making sure the Closing Disclosure is received three days prior to closing on the loan.

Hopefully, the outlines of TRID and the purpose have been adequately explained. This is a new law and to see how well it will work out is something that can only be speculated about. Until history reveals itself in this new 'New Deal', only time will tell.

www.ingramcontent.com/pod-product-compliance
Lightning Source LLC
Chambersburg PA
CBHW070759180526
45168CB00004B/1680